Original title:
Meadow Miracles

Copyright © 2025 Creative Arts Management OÜ
All rights reserved.

Author: Kieran Blackwood
ISBN HARDBACK: 978-1-80567-015-5
ISBN PAPERBACK: 978-1-80567-095-7

The Crescendo of the Meadow

In a field where daisies bow,
The cows debate who's queen of the sow.
A chicken struts, a rooster sings,
While rabbits plot their hidden things.

A grasshopper leaps with a great big grin,
While butterflies dance, oh the chaos begins!
The wind joins in, a playful tease,
Tickling the flowers, shaking the trees.

An errant goat steals a farmer's hat,
While squirrels giggle, as they scatter and chat.
The sun winks down, a smirk on its face,
As clumsy hedgehogs juggle in place.

And when night falls, the owls will cheer,
As fireflies gather, lighting up here.
A concert of chuckles in every nook,
In this place where all nature's a book.

The Hummingbird's Secret

In the garden, a blur flies by,
Wings like laughter, oh my!
Sipping nectar with a grin,
Is that a bee? Or a hummingbird kin?

Echoes in the Ferns

Whispers dance, oh so weird,
Ferns giggle, not a single tear.
What's that rustle? A squirrel's prank,
Or maybe a rabbit in a fancy tank?

Canvas of Color Through the Seasons

Spring's in bloom, colors collide,
Butterflies argue, who'll decide?
Every shade a funky fight,
Daisy's winning, 'cause she's polite!

Flutters of Light in the Meadow

A butterfly flaps with a great show,
"Catch me if you can!" He'd crow.
Meanwhile, bees buzz in a sweet spree,
Plotting how to steal syrupy easy!

Gentle Echoes of Nature

In lush grass, a bee hums loud,
Wearing stripes, feeling quite proud.
A dandelion's fluff takes flight,
Sails off like a kite in the light.

A squirrel dances, quite a show,
Chasing shadows, to and fro.
The sunbeams tickle daisies bright,
As they giggle in sheer delight.

Serenity Among the Stems

A snail in shades, so bold and bright,
Moves at a speed that feels just right.
Each step a miracle, so grand,
As curious ants lend a helping hand.

A ladybug takes off with flair,
Doing loops in the soft, warm air.
A grumpy toad wears a crown of moss,
While chuckling bees buzz at a loss.

Serendipity in Green

A butterfly wears polka dot socks,
Tripping over garden rocks.
While frogs compete with silly songs,
Nature giggles, where fun belongs.

Tall flowers peep, trying to pry,
Secrets of clouds floating by.
A wind gust spins, what a dance!
Caterpillars join, taking a chance.

The Canvas of Spring

Painting blooms with colors bright,
Puppies chase, oh such a sight!
The sun sneezes, oh what a blunder,
Raindrops giggle and roll with thunder.

A worm on a leaf, winks with glee,
Whispers to flowers, "Come play with me!"
Grasshoppers leap in rhythmic cheer,
As nature's laughter fills the sphere.

Beneath the Canopy of Petals

Beneath the blooms, the bees do dance,
They hum a tune, full of romance.
A butterfly sneezes, oh what a sight,
It makes the flowers giggle with delight.

A worm in a tie, he struts with pride,
Claims he's the best in the garden wide.
The daisies snicker, they whisper a joke,
While grass blades giggle at the earth's fine cloak.

Nature's Canvas of Joy

A canvas stretched where colors bloom,
Squirrels in tutus twirl and zoom.
A thistle winks with a prickly smile,
While daisies dance, oh such grace and style.

The sun throws colors like paint in the air,
A jolly old robin begins his flair.
The wind plays pranks, tickles the leaves,
While laughter spreads like woven weaves.

Starlit Bloom

Under twinkling lights, flowers yawn wide,
A snail in pajamas slides down the side.
His shell is shiny, like a crescent moon,
He grins at the stars, humming a tune.

A frog dons glasses, reads poetry loud,
To a chorus of crickets, he feels so proud.
Laughter echoes through the night's embrace,
A garden of dreams, a whimsical place.

Conversations with the Breeze

The breeze comes giggling, a playful tease,
Whispers sweet nothings through the trees.
A dandelion puffs, then rolls with glee,
"Blow me a wish!" it sings to the sea.

The clouds join in, wearing cotton hats,
A party of shadows, while nature chats.
Every gust carries laughter's cheer,
In this comical world, joy is near.

The Language of Trees

In the forest, trees talk loud,
Squirrels sit in a gossip crowd.
They chuckle at the birds that sing,
Sharing secrets of the spring.

Barking trees with knobby knees,
Swapping stories with the breeze.
One trunk says it saw a deer,
Another claims it once met fear.

A branch swings low, just to tease,
Touching hats, forgetting knees.
Acorns fall like little bombs,
Tree-top laughter in their qualms.

When leaves whisper in the night,
You might catch a cheeky sight.
A squirrel dressed up in a tie,
Hitching rides as stars float by.

Secrets Woven in the Grass

The grass is thick, it surely knows,
About the lies that critters pose.
A worm once said it had a dream,
Of flying high, or so it seemed.

Rabbits hop with tales so bold,
Of secret meetings, and treasures told.
They giggle as they sneak and peek,
At ants in suits, so truly sleek.

Dandelions in a huddle converse,
Dreaming wild of their next terse.
One whispers about using hair,
To make a crown, if they dare.

When the wind pulls off their hats,
They tumble, fall, while still like cats.
Each blade sways with a knowing jig,
As laughter drips from every sprig.

Whispers of Blossoms

In the garden, flowers prance,
Each one hoping for a chance.
With petals wide, they play it cool,
Poppy says, "Let's break a rule!"

A daisy winks and starts to spin,
While tulips chuckle, take it in.
"Let's tease the bees!" the roses shout,
As honeycombs begin to pout.

Petunias rally for some fun,
Telling tales of the sun's run.
"Here comes the rain!" one timid bloom
Yells out loud, and scuttles, zoom!

In a swirl of colors bright,
They dance around from morn till night.
Each blossom fluffs its airy hair,
In a twist of spring, without a care.

Dancers on the Breeze

When the wind begins to swirl,
It carries off each little curl.
Dandelions on a wild spree,
Twirl around like they are free.

The butterflies wear sparkly shoes,
Flitting here, they spread the news.
"Join us for a dance so grand,
In the rhythm of the land!"

Breezes giggle, tickle grass,
While bumblebees fly in a class.
They buzz along, with tunes so sweet,
As everyone joins in the beat.

In the air, a joyful chase,
Every critter finds its place.
Leaves applaud with a clapping cheer,
For the dancers spin all year.

Breathless Beauty of the Field

In the field, a flower sneezed,
It shook the bees, quite startled, pleased.
Grasshoppers danced in silly spins,
While ants pondered their daily wins.

A daisy wore a sunhat bright,
Claimed it was the fashion night.
Butterflies launched their runway show,
Wings flapping fast, a breezy flow.

The poppies giggled, turned so red,
As bunnies hopped, they lost their thread.
And daisies chuckled, "What a sight!"
In the sun's gleam, all felt just right.

The Song of the Thrush

A thrush sang loud, went off the charts,
Singing tunes that tickled hearts.
The notes bounced high, then fell like rain,
Each pitch a wacky, joyful strain.

Nearby a snail began to groove,
With slimy moves, the crowd did move.
The daisies swayed, they felt the beat,
While frogs groggily tapped their feet.

As the sun began to set,
The thrush declared he wasn't done yet.
An encore call, a chirpy grace,
In the leafy stage, a happy place.

Petals in the Wind

Petals flew, a flower fight,
Confetti burst, what a delight!
A gust of wind, the tulips twirled,
As daisies dove, their flags unfurled.

The wind was sly, it scooped and dashed,
A shower of colors, all so flashed.
The buttercups laughed till they cried,
While sunflowers winked with pride.

A ladybug tried to catch a ride,
But the breeze just tossed her side to side.
With petals dancing all around,
Who knew such silly joy was found?

A Festival of Blooms

In blooms galore, a party sprung,
With every color, songs were sung.
The roses wore their dancing shoes,
While violets spread the latest news.

A cheerful bee spun around and humed,
All the flowers seemed well-mummed.
Tulips topped with crowns so fine,
Declared, "Let's celebrate, it's party time!"

The gardener joined, with hugs for all,
As blooms embraced, they had a ball.
From daisies wide to lilies tall,
The festival bloomed, a merry call.

Hearts of the Harvest

In fields of green where veggies play,
The carrots dance, hip-hop all day.
Potatoes chuckle from their brown hide,
While radishes blush, trying to slide.

The squash wears glasses, looking quite smart,
Telling corny jokes, a veggie art.
Tomatoes roll in fits of glee,
As pumpkins jockey for their spree.

Each harvest day, a riotous cheer,
With veggies laughing, spreading good cheer.
Cabbages giggle, heads all aglow,
In the patch, it's quite the show!

Even the weeds join in the fun,
They twist and shout, out in the sun.
In hearts of harvest, life's a blast,
Where laughter grows, and joy holds fast.

Revelations Among the Wild

Among the bushes, secrets unfold,
Squirrels gossip, their tales are bold.
A fox in a hat takes a stroll,
While a raccoon surveys his glowing soul.

The birds throw parties, singing all night,
While ladybugs twirl in sheer delight.
Grasshoppers play hide and seek, so sly,
They leap like ninjas, oh me, oh my!

Daisies spin tales of the sun's warm glow,
While ants parade with a garlic clove.
Every corner hides a giggly find,
Wild and wacky, it's quite the bind!

Amidst the wild, life's a grand jest,
Every creature knows it's better to jest.
With laughter echoing through the trees,
Revelations whirl upon the breeze.

Curves of Carefree

Butterflies twist with playful flair,
Flitting around without a care.
Dandelions giggle at the breeze,
Waving their seeds with utmost ease.

A bumblebee winks as he buzzes by,
Chasing a ladybug all through the sky.
While a curious snail makes his slow pass,
Admiring the grass through the tall glass.

The sunflowers stretch, basking in cheer,
While a wily worm draws near.
They twist in circles, full of glee,
In curves of carefree, wild and free.

Nature's dance, a whimsical spree,
Where every twist feels like jubilee.
In this lush world, they spin and twirl,
Sending giggles to every girl and boy!

Nature's Gentle Laboratory

In a lab where flowers wear lab coats,
They mix up potions, oh what floats!
With bees as assistants, buzzing away,
Creating sweet honey, come what may.

The mossy couches hold secret talks,
As critters gather in their froggy crocs.
Researching puddles for the best splash,
Creating ripples, oh what a bash!

The rabbits calculate how to hop,
While turtles ponder if they can stop.
Nature experiments in every nook,
With each little laugh, just take a look!

In this gentle lab of joy and mirth,
Every creature shines, all prove their worth.
A world of wonder, chic and spry,
Where laughter and science soar high!

Lullabies from the Land

In the grass, a tune plays soft,
A frog sings high, a toad jumps off.
The crickets join in, their chirps delight,
As fireflies wink in the fading light.

A bird on a branch has lost its shoe,
Chasing its shadow, it hops and coos.
The sun dips low, as giggles soar,
Nature's laugh echoes, forevermore.

A sleeping cow snores loud and proud,
While ants march on, a bustling crowd.
With dreams of grass, they drift and sway,
Counting the stars till the break of day.

So let the tunes of earth invite,
A laugh, a dance, all through the night.
In this land, where silliness thrives,
The lullabies keep us all alive.

Nectar of the Open Air

Bees in aprons zoom about,
Wearing hats, they dance, no doubt.
Pollinating with glee in sight,
Sipping nectar, oh, what a bite!

A curious bloom waves from afar,
"Try me!" it calls, like a candy bar.
With each petal, a giggle grows,
Sprinkling laughter, it softly glows.

The butterflies wear colors bright,
Flapping their wings, they take a flight.
Stumbling on petals, so clumsy and bold,
Their antics are worth more than gold.

Nature's buffet, so wild and free,
Serves up fun, come taste with me.
With every sip and every cheer,
We savor sweetness, year by year.

The Dance of Insects

A ladybug twirls, oh what grace!
Strutting its spots in a joyful race.
The grasshoppers join with a leap and a bounce,
Each twist and turn makes the flowers flounce.

Ants in a line, they march to the beat,
In search of snacks, they're quick on their feet.
With tiny top hats and tails that swirl,
They're throwing a party, watch them whirl!

A dragonfly dips, then swings 'round a stem,
Wearing a crown, a royal gem.
While beetles tap dance, night on the town,
No need for a stage, just lay the grass down.

Insects unite, it's a vibrant show,
Full of laughter, making joy overflow.
So when you're outside, stop for a glance,
And join in the fun, share a silly dance!

Rustic Revelations

The rooster's crow sounds like a tune,
He's a musician, morning's buffoon.
While cows bicker over the breakfast hay,
A sheep steals the spotlight, what can I say?

A pig in a puddle takes quite a dive,
Snorting with joy, oh how he thrives!
With mud on its face, a true work of art,
A silly spectacle that warms the heart.

Chickens cluck gossip, tales getting wild,
While goats play tag, they're nature's child.
Each little frolic brings giggles to share,
Rustic revelations float on the air.

Join in the laughter, forget all your woes,
In this playful farm where the fun always grows.
For life is a sketch of color and cheer,
It's the rustic charm that makes it so clear.

Whispers of the Wildflowers

In a field where daisies dance,
A bee wore stripes, took a chance.
With each buzz, he told a joke,
The flowers laughed, what a bloke!

Tulips teased the passing breeze,
Said, 'We're too pretty to freeze!'
A dandy lion laughed with glee,
Claimed he was king, as proud as can be!

Buttercups pulled off a prank,
Hiding carrots, oh what a tank!
A rabbit jumped to claim his prize,
Found a flower instead—what a surprise!

Amongst the blooms, a frog did cheer,
Said, 'I'll croak a tune, lend me your ear!'
While crickets chirped in a band so spry,
The wildflowers swayed as time zipped by!

Dreaming Beneath the Sunlit Sky

Beneath the sun, a little snail,
Dreamed of flying, oh, without fail!
Said he'd ride on a butterfly's back,
But got stuck—oh, what a wacky hack!

A grasshopper broke into a song,
Claimed to leap all day long.
But slipped on dew, fell with a thud,
Laughed by flowers—oh! What a dud!

Ladybugs had a fancy soirée,
Dressed in red with a coat of grey.
They ordered nectar, sweet and bright,
But spilled it all, what a silly sight!

The sun smiled wide, watching the show,
Nature's laughter, a lovely glow.
With every giggle shared by all,
The sky echoed—what a playful call!

Dewdrop Serenade

Droplets twinkled on leaves and grass,
Like tiny stars—oh, what a class!
A raindrop fell, started to sing,
A tune so bright, made the flowers swing!

The morning mist joined the fun,
Whispering secrets, one by one.
A caterpillar schmoozed a bumblebee,
'Can I ride? I'll be light as a flea!'

A dragonfly laughed, said with flair,
'You'll be dizzy—full of despair!'
But they danced as sunlight shone,
Nature's laughter—never alone!

So dewdrops glistened, made their way,
Creating music all through the day.
With every drop, a giggling sound,
Life's little treasures all around!

Secrets of the Sunflower Field

In a field where sunflowers play,
One wore shades, enjoying the day.
Claimed it was too bright to see,
'Turn down the sun or let me be!'

A squirrel danced, with acorns to sell,
'Got your tickets for the sunflower swell!'
He tumbled and rolled, all cheeks and fluff,
Said, 'Life is nuts—and that's enough!'

Tall sunflowers swayed with pride,
'We're the stars, come take a ride!'
But when the wind gave a strong blow,
They all wobbled—oh, what a show!

The secret's out, laughter fills the air,
Nature's quirks beyond compare.
With each little chuckle from the field,
Joy unravels, no need to shield!

Radiant Colors of Tranquility

Amidst the greens, the daisies dance,
With butterflies caught in a silly prance.
The sun spills joy in golden streams,
As frogs croak life in their froggy dreams.

A patch of red makes the squirrels laugh,
While rabbits munch on a leafy half.
The sky wears blue like grandma's curl,
As dance-offs break out in a twirly swirl.

The clouds do backflips, the grass whispers fun,
A riot of colors, oh, what a run!
In this laughter-filled, leafy space,
Nature winks with a giddy face.

So if you stumble on laughter's spree,
Join in the fun, oh, don't just see!
With colors bright like a playful jest,
In nature's arms, we are truly blessed.

A Symphony of Serenity

The crickets chirp in a comical tune,
As raccoons and owls dance under the moon.
The breeze carries notes from a bubbling brook,
Where fish wear hats and take a good look.

A soft tune plays as flowers sway,
While ladybugs gossip about the day.
The rabbits juggle acorns on high,
And grasshoppers leap like they could fly.

Each rustle and giggle, a melody bright,
With nature's own band playing all night.
A symphony made of laughter and cheer,
In this happy green theatre, all is clear.

So come take a seat in the front row seat,
Where frogs are the stars and bugs bring the beat.
In this grand concert, where joy won't cease,
Nature sings softly, a song of peace.

The Gentle Heart of the Landscape

A butterfly flutters on softest wings,
While the young grass makes giggly springs.
An ant's on a quest with a crumb in tow,
In this fun-filled place where all creatures go.

The daisies debate on who's the best,
While dandelions challenge with cheeky jest.
A snail with sunglasses struts through the grass,
With a smile that says, 'You'll never surpass!'

Clouds play peek-a-boo in the sky so blue,
While shadows frolic, giving life a view.
Each sunset's hue wraps around like a hug,
Where painted horizons make hearts feel snug.

So frolic and laugh in this land so grand,
Join in the fun, take a leap with the sand.
For in this heart, where smiles bloom wide,
Nature invites you to dance and glide.

Where Bees Write Poetry

In a world where bees compose from the hive,
Their verses flutter and buzz, come alive.
With tiny quills dipped in honeyed bliss,
They scribble sweet lines that I can't miss.

The flowers applaud with petals so bright,
As poetry swirls in the warm sunlight.
A bumblebee poet recites with delight,
While butterflies spin tales in graceful flight.

Grass tickles toes as I laugh and sway,
At the curious critters who waltz and play.
Each line a tickle, each rhyme a smile,
In this flowering book, let's stay awhile.

So let's join the verse in this playful spree,
Where laughter and nature blend joyfully.
For life's a sweet poem, a whimsical beat,
In this buzzing romance, we all find our seat.

The Generosity of Green

In the patch of grass, a worm is found,
Wiggling with glee, it's dancing around.
The daisies are laughing, they sway in delight,
Saying, "Join in the fun, it's such a fine sight!"

A squirrel named Barry with acorn in hand,
Tripped on a root, oh, wasn't it grand!
He rolled past the daisies and bumped into trees,
"Next time I'll watch where I'm going," he teases.

The wind blows a tune, a soft silly sound,
It tickles the flowers, they giggle profound.
Bees buzzing loudly, make mischief today,
Stealing sweet nectar, in a comical way!

A rabbit in bowtie and tiny top hat,
Jumps over daisies, looking quite fat.
He bows to the crowd with a flourish and spin,
"Oh, thank you! Thank you!" as he lands with a grin.

Nature's Gentle Hand

A bee on a mission, wearing a frown,
Landed on fussy petals, causing a gown.
"Oh dear!" cried the flower, "That's not the way,
You're ruining my look; I have dinner today!"

The buttercups whispered, "It's tough being bright,
We attract every bug, oh what a plight!
We shine like the sun, but goodness, we share,
With critters that linger and pull at our hair!"

A snail with a monocle crossed on his path,
Took time for a moment to calculate math.
"Two plus two equals—wait, is that a leaf?
Oh laws, I forgot!" He sighed in disbelief.

The grass plays a tune, it sways with the breeze,
Tickling some bunnies, they giggle with ease.
Nature has tricks, and oh the delight,
Who knew a green patch could be this polite?

Threads of Tranquility

A spider's web glimmered, what a sight to see,
"Do you think I'm a chandelier?" quipped the bee.
With sparkles and glints, she felt quite divine,
"Now don't mess this up! It's my moment to shine!"

The clouds overhead wore a fluffy white guise,
Floating carelessly with lazy surprise.
"Is today a good day for a nap in the breeze?
I'll count all the sheep—uh oh, where's my cheese?"

A fox strolled by, with a snicker and grin,
"I'm stealthy, I'm sly!" he declared with a spin.
But tripped on a root—it was a laughable tumble,
"Who knew grass could be such a daring old jumble?"

The sunset brought red, orange, and hues of pure gold,
As raccoons planned dinner, "Are we eating cold?"
"Just grab all the snacks!" one cheekily said,
"Don't worry, my friends, it's just dinner in bed!

Echoes of a Spring Day

The woodpecker knocked on an old wrinkled tree,
"Excuse me, good sir, can you keep it down, please?"
The tree just chuckled, "Oh what do you mean?
This is my best bongo, like you've never seen!"

A ladybug twirled on a leaf in the sun,
"I'm dancing, I'm dancing! Oh, isn't this fun?"
But slipped on a dewdrop, splashing down fast,
"Excuse me, dear leaf, I'm not built for a blast!"

The clouds formed a dragon, all fluffy and grand,
"Let's soar through the sky, just give me a hand!"
But the wind wasn't happy, it gave them a shove,
"Not on my watch, I'm the one that they love!"

As day fades to evening, the stars start to gleam,
"Are we having a picnic?" asked a gleeful stream.
"Bring all the snacks, we'll feast till we pop,
Then giggle with fireflies until we all drop!"

A Quiet Kind of Joy

In fields where daisies dance and play,
A rabbit trips, what a funny display!
With every hop, a giggle breaks free,
As butterflies tease, oh, can't you see?

A snail on a race, who would have thought?
With slime trails left behind, he's caught!
And cows that moo in rhythmic delight,
Bring laughter alive in the warm, golden light.

Worms sing songs as they wiggle around,
While ants march on, they're homeward bound!
A pig in a puddle, splashing with glee,
Makes everyone smile, it's plain to see!

So laugh with the critters, join the fun spree,
In this quirky haven, so wild and free!
With each little moment, we find such joy,
In nature's comedy, there's naught to annoy!

Vibrations of Vibrancy

Dandelions wear hats of bright sunny cheer,
As bees buzz by, 'Hey, let's all gather here!'
The grass whispers secrets, a ticklish affair,
While ladybugs twirl in the warm summer air.

A frog on a lily, he thinks he's a star,
Ribbits his heart out, a real avatar!
While caterpillars don't know their fate,
"Will I fly high or just be late?"

A stream gurgles laughter, it splashes around,
While fish make a splash, a carnival sound!
Each glance at the squirrels, they're playing their game,
With antics so silly, it's hard to explain!

Flowers gossip about who wears the best bloom,
And the sun winks down, lighting up the whole room!
In this vibrant chaos, a party takes flight,
In the heart of the fields, everything's just right!

The Legacy of Laughter

A goat on a hill, thinks he's a big shot,
But stumbles and tumbles right down with a plop!
The sheep roll their eyes, they've seen all his tricks,
While the rooster crows loud, "Let's all have some kicks!"

Old trees tell tales of giggles and fun,
As squirrels play tag, 'til the day is done!
With acorns as treasures, they race with great zest,
It's a comedy show, oh, who's the best?

The wind carries laughter, a breezy delight,
As clouds play peek-a-boo; what a silly sight!
We'll dance with the daisies, and skip on our way,
With nature's own chuckles, chasing worries away!

Each chuckle a memory, each smile a step,
In fields full of joy, our hearts intercept!
So join in the laughter, it's quite the grand ball,
In this playful kingdom, there's room for us all!

Interludes of Illumination

A firefly flickers, a lamp with no shade,
It giggles and wiggles, a bright serenade!
While crickets compose a raucous night song,
The stars join the chorus, it won't be long.

A hedgehog in glasses, reads under a tree,
A novel on worms, what a sight to see!
With every turn of the page, there's a snicker,
As porcupines play pranks—oh, they sure are quick!

Mice throw a feast, with cheese as the treat,
While owls in their wisdom enjoy the sweet beat!
Each cheeky exchange is a wonder to hear,
In the twilight's embrace, we shed every fear.

So gather the creatures, let laughter abound,
In this spectacle of light, joy is found!
In these interludes glimmering, precious and bright,
Let's dance through the night, under soft, glowing light!

Journey Through the Blooming Vale

In a vale where blooms all shout,
Bees with tiny boots run about.
A frog in a tuxedo takes a leap,
While daisies giggle, oh so deep.

A snail with dreams of being fast,
Joins the race, but finishes last.
Butterflies in shades of the sun,
Play hopscotch, oh what silly fun!

Chirping crickets throw a bash,
With acorn hats and food to stash.
Each flower brings a silly smile,
As laughter echoes for a mile.

In the end, the sun dips low,
A jolly scene, a bright hello.
Nighttime stars begin to prance,
In this vale, they join the dance.

Nature's Tapestry Unfurled

A canvas bright, with hues and tones,
Where squirrels sing and dance on stones.
The trees wear hats of leafy green,
While raccoons plot their mischief scheme.

A butterfly with spots like cheese,
Flutters down, it's sure to tease.
A caterpillar's aiming high,
But trips on roots and takes to sky.

The brook, it gurgles, laughs for days,
As fish perform their silly ways.
Frogs with shades that flash and gleam,
Join in the water's playful dream.

The sun sets low, a golden hue,
Nature waves, "We're done, adieu!"
But in this stripe of wild delight,
Laughter lingers through the night.

The Dance of Daisies

Daisies twirl in breezy spins,
While grasshoppers make sly grins.
A ladybug in polka dots,
Claims the stage, and jokes a lot.

The wind blows by with snickers sound,
As petals swirl and twirl around.
A dancing ant with tiny shoes,
Steals the show, but has to lose.

Sunlight sheets on furry bugs,
Who hiss and hum like tiny jugs.
A merry scene, oh what a sight,
When nature laughs from morn to night.

With moon above, the giggles grow,
As stars wink down, the night-time show.
In this dance of floral cheer,
Silly joys are ever near.

In the Shade of Willow Dreams

In willows where the shadows play,
Squirrels scurry, overhear the fray.
A picnic spread, but ants invade,
In search of crumbs that never fade.

A rabbit dons a tiny hat,
Picketing against the old sly cat.
Their quarrels bubble into cheer,
As laughter resonates quite clear.

Fireflies wear their glowing gear,
A dance-off starts, the rules unclear.
With each blink, they bring a grin,
Who knew the fun could thus begin?

When twilight falls, and tales are spun,
The joyful critters, all in one.
In the shade where wonders bloom,
Every giggle chases gloom.

Beneath the Canopy of Colors

Beneath a rainbow high and bright,
The flowers dance in pure delight.
A sunflower winks, what a tease!
While daisies giggle in the breeze.

The sky's a canvas, shades galore,
While ants hold dance-offs on the floor.
Butterflies flutter, give a cheer,
As crickets wear shades, looking dear.

Ladybugs laugh, a sight to see,
Telling tales of their big spree.
"Did you hear? The grasshoppers sing!"
Spreading gossip on little wings.

Oh, what fun in this realm so bright,
Where bees buzz tales of sheer delight.
Every petal, a joke or a tease,
Nature's circus, perfect with ease.

Woven Tapestries of Life

In threads of green, we weave our fun,
With every bloom, a story's spun.
The toads perform their nightly song,
While fireflies flash, it won't be long.

A butterfly calls, "Join my parade!"
While shadows dance in the cool shade.
Each leaf a friend, a hearty cheer,
As frogs play hopscotch, never fear.

The rabbits hop with hats so grand,
Spinning tales of their travel band.
"Who wore it best?" a squirrel will ask,
While nature's critters don their masks.

So gather close, enjoy the show,
Where laughter blooms and breezes blow.
In this tapestry, pure delight,
Life's a jest, from morn to night.

Trinkets in the Grass

Look closely now, what do you see?
A shiny rock, could it be glee?
A ladybug with spotted flair,
Says, "Stop and smile, come join the fair!"

A treasure hunt beneath your feet,
Where beetles march with tiny beat.
Each clover holds a secret rare,
While ants parade without a care.

A dandelion, the king of jest,
Turns wishes into quite the test.
As children giggle, hair a mess,
Imagining all things to confess.

So pick a flower, make it bright,
Share a laugh beneath the light.
For in this grass, so full of fun,
Life's little trinkets have begun.

Abundance of the Earth

The earth provides, a buffet wide,
Where veggies play a game of hide.
A pumpkin hides behind the kale,
While carrots boast they never fail.

In gardens bright with laughter loud,
The tomatoes wear a juicy shroud.
While cucumbers giggle in their rows,
And radishes wear funny clothes.

Mushrooms sprout with silly hats,
Waving to the clever rats.
"Let's throw a feast, what do you think?"
They gather round with glasses clink.

So raise a toast to greens and beans,
To nature's quirks and playful scenes.
In this abundance, joy's unearthed,
Life's a party, full of mirth!

Flourishing Through Time

In the field where the daisies dance,
The butterflies throw a goofy glance.
Bumblebees buzz with a silly tune,
As grasshoppers hold a hopping boon.

A squirrel slides down a leafy slide,
While giggling flowers stand side by side.
Thistle tries to be the lady's maid,
But bursts out laughing, just can't be swayed.

With every breeze, tales blow and sway,
The trees tell jokes in a leafy way.
Laughter echoes in this green space,
As sunbeams tickle each furry face.

Time waltzes on with a clumsy grip,
While rabbits make a ticklish trip.
In this wild spot, joy finds a spark,
And giggles bloom with a sneaky lark.

The Language of Vines

Vines twist up with secrets to share,
While pumpkins giggle, all round and fair.
The cucumber whispers to the shy pea,
'Let's have a party by the old tree!'

Grapes roll down, making quite the scene,
Dressed in green, looking very keen.
Lettuce laughs at the tomato's plight,
As they toss seeds in a playful fight.

In this garden, all under the sun,
Nature's riddle is a ton of fun.
Each leaf and stem tells a quirky tale,
With giggles and snorts on a breezy trail.

Tangled in laughter, vines share their lore,
As veggies dance on the garden floor.
Listen closely to the roots and shoots,
For the best jokes come in fuzzy boots!

A Tapestry of Tranquil Thoughts

A blanket spread on the grass so green,
Where ants march in like a funny scene.
Clouds drift by with a whimsical grin,
While the sun plays peekaboo from within.

The daisies pose in comical rows,
Sticking out tongues at the prancing crows.
Butterflies wiggle, all dressed in charm,
Making flowers blush with their silly arm.

A soft breeze tickles the willow's hair,
As squirrels rehearse their tightrope stare.
In this quiet quilt of laughter and cheer,
Each moment spins into a joyful sphere.

The chirps of the crickets add to the fun,
While shadows flicker as day's nearly done.
In this serene spot where thoughts unwind,
A tapestry of laughter is what we find.

Reverberations in Petals

In fields adorned with colors bright,
Petals giggle in the warm sunlight.
Tulips prance with a funny flair,
As daisies whisper jokes in the air.

Bees wearing hats come buzzing round,
With punchlines that never fail to astound.
Poppies sway to the jester's tune,
While the daisies chuckle, 'Must be afternoon!'

With every sway, a new pun is made,
Nature's comedy show never does fade.
Grass sways like it's laughing out loud,
Making the flowers dance in a crowd.

The sun dips down, casting a glow,
Where petals hum their sweet little flow.
In this delightful, funny display,
Nature's laughter lights up the way.

Kisses of the Sun

A warm hug from above, so bright,
Bees dance wildly, what a sight!
Grass tickles toes, never shy,
As ants parade by, oh my!

Sun hats perched at silly angles,
Flip-flops flop as the breeze wrangles.
Laughter scatters like dandelion seeds,
Nature's jesters fulfill our needs.

A squirrel juggles acorns with flair,
While clouds play hide-and-seek in the air.
Each ray a giggle, each shadow a sigh,
Under this canopy, we dance and fly.

A lemonade stand run by a snail,
Sips so slow, we can't help but wail.
In every moment, a laugh to be shared,
Kisses from above, nothing else compared.

Conversations with the Wind

The breeze whispers secrets to the trees,
While birds gossip over teas and cheeses.
With every gust, a joke takes flight,
As butterflies prank through the bright sunlight.

Winds play tug-of-war with hats,
Stealing away from chattering chitchats.
They tease the flowers to sway and dance,
Setting nature's stage for a silly prance.

Clouds eavesdrop on the sun's jokes,
While rabbits roll, telling puns like folks.
With every whoosh, a tickle in the air,
Who knew such laughter could be everywhere?

And if you listen close, you'll hear
The wind's laughter soft, yet clear.
In the rustling leaves, a tale spins round,
In the theater of green, joy is found.

Radiance in Every Ray

Light beams bounce with a giggle and gleam,
As shadows play hide-and-seek in a stream.
Each flicker of sunlight winks at a bee,
With fireflies joining in playful glee.

The daisies crack jokes to the bumblebees,
While sunflowers sway, swaying with ease.
A glow of laughter fills the bright air,
With rainbow colors, it's beyond compare.

Here, even clouds wear a silly face,
As they drift along in a lazy race.
The horizon blushes, a giggly red,
While light bounces off giggles that spread.

Every ray has a story to tell,
A shimmering joke in this sunlit shell.
In the theater of brightness, we play today,
In a spectrum of joy, we bask and sway.

Chasing Hues

Colors chase each other, a playful race,
As blues tickle greens, oh what a grace!
Pinks and yellows swirl in delight,
Creating a canvas that's out of sight.

The orange crayon slipped on the grass,
While violet giggles just didn't pass.
A palette of laughter burst in the day,
In a world of hues where we love to play.

Each flower a burst of cheeky surprise,
While color battles bloom like butterflies.
Daisies dab yellow on a cheeky blue,
In this playful landscape, laughter renews.

As dusk brings purple, the sun bids adieu,
With twinkles of stars, a colorful crew.
In every shade, there's a smile to chase,
In this world of wonder, we find our place.

Awe in Every Blade

In a field so green and wide,
Ants march like they own the tide.
Grasshoppers hop in silly ways,
Waving at clouds that need a shave.

A butterfly wearing shoes of lace,
Dancing with bees in a fuzzy race.
They giggle and twirl in the sunny light,
Whispering secrets to the tired kite.

Beneath the daisies, rabbits scheme,
Planning a picnic; oh, what a dream!
But all they get is a pack of flies,
Who bring the cake but eat the pies!

So next time you stroll where flowers bloom,
Remember the fun in nature's room.
Each blade of grass has a tale to tell,
Of laughter and joy that we know so well.

Horizon of Serenity

The sky wears a hat of smirking blue,
While clouds play tag; oh, what a view!
Squirrels debate on the best acorn,
While trying to dodge a rogue unicorn.

The flowers dance in a conga line,
Their petals fluffier than a pillow divine.
They giggle so loud, they wake up the bees,
Who wear tiny hats and sip on their teas.

A dandelion wishes upon a breeze,
Blowing its seeds with hilarious ease.
They float like balloons pretending to fly,
While critters below all just roll with a sigh.

The horizon chuckles, a vast open space,
Holding the echoes of nature's embrace.
In all the chaos, find your own cheer,
And laugh with the world, for it's all so dear.

Embracing the Earth

The ground's a couch for the ants and fleas,
Underneath trees that dance in the breeze.
A worm pops out with a curious grin,
Saying, "Come sit! The fun's about to begin!"

A ladybug decked in spots of red,
Claims that she's queen of the garden bed.
But the caterpillar rolls his eyes so wide,
Saying, "Dear lady, you missed the ride!"

Crickets chirp in a symphony mad,
With a frog who thinks he's the best he's had.
Together they shout in a cacophony bright,
Creating a concert till the fall of night.

The earth wraps us all in a cozy embrace,
With laughter and silliness woven in space.
So kick off your shoes, feel the grass 'neath your feet,
And join nature's party; it's quite the treat!

Colors of Cheer

Red poppies giggle, yellow pansies sing,
While purple violets do a happy swing.
Each petal whispers a joke or two,
Tickling the dew with laughter anew.

A rainbow sneezes, sending colors around,
As sunbeams giggle upon the ground.
The grass tries to mimic a disco ball,
Wobbling in rhythm; it's having a ball!

Bumblebees waltz, buzzing 'round with flair,
While butterflies flutter as if they don't care.
It's a colorful mess, yet a beautiful sight,
Turning the dull into pure delight.

So wear your smile like a flower in bloom,
Spread laughter and joy, chase away gloom.
For in every color, in every cheer,
There's magic to find when laughter is near.

Spirit of the Blossom

A dandelion wishes it could fly,
But its friends just laugh and ask it why.
"You're too bright to leave this patch,
Stay here, dear pal, let's make a match!"

A bumblebee buzzing with style and grace,
Dances round flowers in a frenzied chase.
"Stop chasing me!" the petal shouts loud,
As the buzzing crowd forms a little cloud.

A ladybug jokes, "I've got spots to spare!"
While caterpillars munch without a care.
"You're all so silly, let's have a race!"
So they zoom on leaves, full of laughter and grace.

In this lively patch where colors collide,
Nature's comedians take it all in stride.
With giggles and tickles, the sunshine beams—
Life is just fun, the garden's alive with dreams!

The Brushstrokes of Dawn

The sun peeks out, chasing shadows away,
While the rooster's alarm screams, "It's a new day!"
A squirrel jumps high, looks silly and spry,
"I'm practicing flying! Just watch me try!"

The painter's brush flings colors galore,
As blossoms burst open, and bees start to soar.
"Hey, who dropped my paint?" the butterfly sighs,
"It's not on my wings; it's stuck to my eyes!"

The grass tickles toes, a delicate tease,
While ants hold a meeting beneath the oak trees.
"What's this about grapes?" a snail starts to muse,
"All I want is a meal or maybe some snooze!"

As daisies chuckle and violets hum,
Nature's a circus; it's all such great fun!
In the palette of morning, let laughter unfurl,
Every petal and leaf brings joy to the world!

The Carousel of Creation

The wind blows in, giving flowers a spin,
While the daisies giggle, they're ready to win.
"Let's get this party started!" a tulip calls out,
As the petals all twirl and the bees dance about.

A ladybug twirls in a dazzling skirt,
While caterpillars watch and wave in the dirt.
"Join us! Join us!" the flowers all cheer,
But the ants just grumble, for they're stuck in gear.

A sunbeam whirls 'round, tickling leaves,
"Come join the dance! I've got tricks up my sleeves!"
The butterflies giggle, take flight with a prance,
While the shadows just grump, missing this chance.

In the circus of colors, it's hard not to grin,
As petals do pirouettes, let the laughter begin.
With each bright rotation, creation's alive,
In this playground of joy, everything can thrive!

Tides of Tranquility

The babbling brook sings a silly song,
While frogs in the shade croak along all day long.
"Jump in! Jump in!" the minnows all tease,
But the turtles just yawn, as they doze in the breeze.

Crickets are drumming a rhythmic beat,
While the fireflies blink, oh so sweet.
"Are we on stage?" a grasshopper shouts,
As the night air fills up with giggles and doubts.

A hedgehog rolls by, all prickly and round,
While the raccoons chuckle at the funny sound.
"Hey, watch me skate!" says a bold little mouse,
As she twirls on the path, out front of her house.

In the glow of the moon, all nature's delight,
Laughter and whispers make everything bright.
These tides of glee flow with murmurs so sweet,
In the heart of the night, where joy's sure to meet!

Fleeting Moments of Bliss

Bumblebees buzz with a glee,
While ants march on like they own the spree.
A ladybug laughs, oh what a show,
Wearing polka dots like a funky pro.

Grasshopper plays his tiny flute,
Singing to daisies, oh how cute!
A pickle jar rolls down the hill,
Chasing a squirrel with a flair for thrill.

The Mirage of Color

Buttercups dance in a dizzy whirl,
While rainbow ribbons begin to twirl.
A butterfly slips on its new shoes,
And lands in the grass like it's got the blues.

Frogs compete in a leap race,
Hopping high, they're setting the pace.
With splashes of water, they call it a day,
And lounge on lily pads, hip-hip-hooray!

Reflections in the Dew

Morning dew shines like little stars,
On grass blades sparkling, not too far.
A snail slides through with such great pride,
Wearing a shell that's a slight bit wide.

A mouse plays peek-a-boo with a cat,
Squeaking loudly, "Can you handle that?"
But the cat just yawns, quite unimpressed,
While the mouse winks, feeling quite blessed.

Enchantment in the Air

Winds blow softly, carrying tales,
Of dancing flowers and little snails.
A pigeon jokes with a perky crow,
About the best places to steal the show.

The sun winks down, a cheeky sight,
As shadows play tag, what a delight!
And daisies chuckle, swaying about,
As butterflies puff, with a "look at me" shout.

The Butterfly's Dance

A butterfly swayed on a tall dandelion,
Wearing polka dots, just like a lion.
It tried to impress with a twirl and a dip,
But tripped on a flower and took a quick slip.

The beetles all giggled, they rolled on the ground,
'Can you believe it? That move was profound!'
But the butterfly laughed, with a wink and a cheer,
'At least I'm the one with no fear of a sneer!'

The ladybugs clapped, they chanted in rhyme,
'Dance again, oh fluttering friend, it's your time!'
So back to the stage, with a spin and a leap,
The meadow was buzzing; the silliness deep.

With laughter and jigs, the sun shone so bright,
Each creature agreed, it was quite the delight.
To dance is to falter, to laugh is to glide,
In this flurry of joy, no one's left to chide.

Echoes of the Grassland

In the grassland a frog made a blundering croak,
Echoing sweetly like a delightful joke.
His friends all erupted, their giggles took flight,
As he leapt with a hop, a comical sight.

A rabbit heard echoes of laughter and cheer,
He dashed through the clovers, his nose twitching near.
Seeing the fun, he couldn't help but prance,
Joining the frog in an impromptu dance.

Then came a wise owl, all feathered and grand,
With a serious face, about to take a stand.
But upon hearing the froggy refrain,
Even he chuckled and forgot all his reign.

With echoes of joy that swirled all around,
The grassland was filled with soft giggles unbound.
Laughter is music, and what a sweet band,
In the heart of the field, oh so wonderfully planned.

Petals on the Wandering Breeze

Petals were swirling, a curious sight,
Caught in the breeze, a feathery flight.
They danced with such glee, in a whirlwind of flair,
One landed on a hedgehog, what a surprise there!

The hedgehog just chuckled, 'Is this a new style?'
His friends cackled loudly, that prickly old pile.
With each gust of wind, more petals took flight,
Painting the woodland with colors so bright.

A squirrel joined in, head bobbing with beat,
He tried to keep up, but got stuck on his feet.
He spun and he tumbled, creating a mess,
But laughter erupted, 'Oh, what a success!'

With a sprinkle of petals, both big and quite small,
Each found their own rhythm, answering the call.
Together they crafted the silliest spree,
What joy in this dance, oh so wild and so free!

Hidden Treasures of the Green

Amidst the tall grasses, a treasure was found,
A shoelace, a button, all strewn on the ground.
A mouse held a council, 'What can we do?'
They schemed and they plotted, oh what fun they drew!

The rabbit proposed, with a wink and a nod,
'Let's make a grand necklace from what we have trod!
With buttons and shoelaces, a fashion so fine,
We'll win all the critters' applause, all in time!'

The hedgehog wore one, all tangled and wild,
The other critters giggled, some thought him reviled.
But he strutted with pride, oh, what a charade,
Turning heads as he marched, in his button parade!

With laughter abounding, they danced under trees,
Fashioned in nonsense, with smiles and with ease.
For treasures are hidden in places unseen,
Especially in laughter, the finest of glean.

Emotions in Bloom

In the field where daisies giggle,
Butterflies dance, oh what a wiggle!
Bees wear hats made of pollen dust,
As flowers argue, whom to trust.

A tumbleweed rolls, quite the sight,
Shouting at clouds, 'You're too polite!'
Grasshoppers play the banjo in tune,
Croaking frogs sing 'Under the Moon.'

Sunflowers turn, not to just the sun,
But to gossip, oh this is fun!
With every petal, a secret spread,
Who knew flowers had so much said?

In this silly world, joy blooms wide,
Nature's laughter, we can't hide.
With each playful breeze that sweeps,
Even the stumps are doing leaps!

Elysian Fields Calling

In fields so bright, the rabbits hop,
Playing chess, they never stop!
With carrots for pawns, oh what a game,
Claiming victory, but who's to blame?

The daisies wear glasses, sophisticated looks,
Comparing roots like fancy books.
While ladybugs gossip, perched on a leaf,
Spinning tales of joy and grief.

The wind tickles the hay's funny bones,
Grass sways gently, like it's on phones.
'Hello!' says a breeze, with a cheeky wink,
Making daisies blush, oh how they think!

This place is a riot, laughter galore,
With nature's humor, you can't ignore.
A party unfolds, with each joyful bloom,
In fields of delight, there's never gloom!

The Flicker of Light Through Leaves

Sunlight plays peekaboo, oh how it shines,
While squirrels plan their acorn heists and lines.
A shadow darts; it's just a shy snail,
Who dreams of speed, but ends up frail.

Leaves are winking, what a silly sight,
Telling tree tales all through the night.
Mice in hats hold a soirée grand,
With crumbs on the floor, oh isn't it bland?

The breeze adds spice, tickles the grass,
While butterflies argue who's got more sass.
With every flutter, giggles erupt,
Even drab mushrooms join in the fun, oh yes!

And as dusk settles, it's a dance of delight,
Nature's punchlines always ignite.
With laughter in shadows, joy in the trees,
This land of quirkiness fills us with ease!

Grace in Every Stem

In a garden where giggles grow tall,
Tulips wear caps, having a ball.
With whispers of wind, petals begin,
Chasing each other, it's a floral spin!

A lettuce sings, oh what a tune,
Under the light of a cotton candy moon.
While weeds play tag with each passing bee,
Nature's orchestra, oh what glee!

Buttercups blush when the sun comes near,
Declaring, 'We're the prettiest here!'
The peonies chuckle in gentle sway,
As butterflies laugh and dance away.

In every corner, mischief abounds,
A joyful chorus of silly sounds.
With grace in their stems, they sway and lean,
In this paradise, all's merry and green!

A Tapestry of Buttercups

In a field of flashy gold,
Butterflies dance, oh so bold.
They trip on petals, take a dive,
These bouncing critters feel alive.

The daisies giggle, what a sight,
As bees in hats zoom left and right.
They hold a party, all in bloom,
With pollen cakes, they clear the room.

A snail in slippers slowly slides,
While ladybugs roll with pride.
A caterpillar sings a tune,
Wearing sunglasses, looking cool.

As the sun sets, they bid adieu,
Tomorrow brings a brand new crew.
In this quirky carnival of hue,
Laughter echoes, bright and true.

Fragile Beauty in the Shade

Under a tree, where shadows play,
A squirrel shows off in a silly way.
It scampers up, it scampers down,
The jester of the leafy crown.

Lush ferns whisper secrets low,
While a lazy beetle puts on a show.
Winking at flowers, oh how they tease,
"Join us for tea! We're sipping with ease!"

A curious rabbit winks with glee,
As butterflies spin around a tree.
With every flutter, a giggle grows,
Ticklish grass sways, high and low.

In this haven, silliness reigns,
As laughter dances in soft, bright chains.
Nature's jesters, a comic parade,
Celebrate beauty, never afraid.

When Time Stops to Smell the Flowers

A lazy bumblebee drops by,
Wearing a tie, oh my, oh my!
He checks his watch, it's flower time,
Buzzing with glee, all in their prime.

A dandelion in a crown of fluff,
Says, "Blown away? That's just enough!"
While clovers chuckle; they feel elite,
In a patchwork quilt, they shuffle their feet.

The sun yawns wide, a sleepy glow,
Daisies dance in the breezy flow.
They share giggles with leaves above,
In this garden of fun, oh, do we love!

Time unwinds in a playful twist,
Flowers laugh, then they're dismissed.
When each petal falls, it's not the end,
Just nature's way to curve and bend.

A Dance of Shadows and Light

In a swirl of green, shadows skip,
While the sunlight takes a tiny trip.
A shadow pursues, then leaps away,
Frolicking in a bright ballet.

The grass waves back, a mirthful cheer,
As crickets tap dance, "We're almost here!"
While the sun tucks in its flaming ray,
The moon peeks out, joining the play.

Frogs put on masks, a grand charade,
Kicking up splashes, unafraid.
"Oops!" they croak, as puddles soar,
In their little world, they always explore.

So let's twirl under the starlit skies,
Where every shadow holds a surprise.
In this revelry, we share delight,
In the dance of shadows, wrapped in light.

Anemone's Embrace

In pink and purple dresses twirl,
Anemones dance with a giggle and whirl.
Buzzy bees join with a clumsy flight,
Catching the petals, oh what a sight!

A sneaky snail slips on dew,
While butterflies sip on sweet flower brew.
The breeze teases grass, makes it bow,
All the plants are laughing, don't know how!

Daisies play tag with clover and thyme,
They tickle the roots, never care for rhyme.
A roly-poly rolls right by,
Exclaiming, "I'm winning!" with a tiny sigh!

By sunset, the blooms begin to rest,
Yet they still whisper jokes, they jest.
Under the stars they chuckle and freeze,
"Tomorrow, let's prank the slow-poke bees!"

Starlit Wildflower Night

Under the sky with a shimmer so bright,
Wildflowers giggle at the moon's light.
With fireflies playing hide and seek,
The petals dance freely, with laughter unique!

A dandelion starts a joke on a breeze,
Telling tall tales to the sway of trees.
The crickets join in with their chirpy cheer,
While a night owl hoots, "I can't stay near!"

Tulips in pajamas, dreaming away,
Muttering secrets of the sun's ray.
They wake to the sound of a raccoon's snore,
Claiming the night is their favorite chore!

As dawn tiptoes in with a yawning delight,
All the flowers giggle, goodnight to the night.
"We'll be back soon, our colors so bright,
With every sunset, we'll have more delight!"

Guardians of the Glade

In the glade, guards of mischief convene,
With hats made of leaves, it's quite the scene.
Squirrels in armor, so ready to play,
Defending their acorns in a crazy way!

Mushrooms stand tall with a serious face,
"Who stole our sunshine? This is not grace!"
The hedgehogs chuckle, rolling nearby,
"Just follow the laughter; it's hard to deny!"

A wise old toad croaks out some news,
"Just let them be, it's all playful blues!"
The sunflowers nod with a sunny grin,
"Let joy be the battle we happily win!"

As twilight approaches, they set down their pails,
And giggles arise like the evening trails.
For in the glade, laughter reigns supreme,
Where every odd moment is a magical dream!

The Breath of Clovers

In a patch of clovers, oh what a sight,
The four-leaf wonders giggle with delight.
Wiggly worms do a jig in the dirt,
While beetles debate who'll wear the best shirt!

A hare hops by, with a curious glance,
And stumbles right into a clover dance.
The gnomes swap tales on a mossy old log,
"Let's crown the queen!" they laugh with a smog!

The morning dew clinks like glasses of cheer,
While a ladybug sings, "Come gather near!"
They share silly stories that twist and twine,
Under the warm sun, each moment divine!

As dusk draws near, they twirl on a breeze,
Clover hearts laughing like leaves on the trees.
"Tomorrow," they chant, "let's do it again,
For every adventure is sure to gain!"

www.ingramcontent.com/pod-product-compliance
Lightning Source LLC
Chambersburg PA
CBHW071849160426
43209CB00003B/478